Rainbows, Head Lice, and Pea-Green Tile

by Brod Bagert

Illustrated by Kim Doner

POEMS IN THE VOICE OF THE CLASSROOM TEACHER

MAUPIN HOUSE

Published by Maupin House Publishing, Inc.
2416 NW 71 Place
Gainesville, FL 32653

```
        Library of Congress Cataloging-in-Publication Data


Bagert, Brod.
    Rainbows, head lice, and pea-green tile : poems in the voice of
 the classroom teacher / by Brod Bagert ; illustrated by Kim Doner.
      p.   cm.
    ISBN 0-929895-28-2
    1. School children Poetry.  2. Classrooms Poetry.  3. Education
 Poetry.  4. Teachers Poetry.  5. Schools Poetry.   I. Title.
 PS3552.A336R35   1999
 811'.54--dc21                                          99-20003
                                                            CIP
```

First Edition, 1999
Reprinted 2001, 2003, 2004, 2008
Book Designed by Kim Doner
Typeset by Maria Messenger
The text of this book is set in 13.5-point Berkeley Book
The illustrations are done in colored pencil and charcoal

For more information about language arts resources, contact Maupin House:
www.maupinhouse.com
1-800-524-0634

Printed in China through Colorcraft Ltd., Hong Kong

Thank You

I'd like to give a "brod" wink to Mr. Bagert for the pleasure of illustrating his wonderful poems, and a gigantic thank you to my matchmakers, Lucie Smith, Rachel Bess, and Anna Wilson, along with the exemplary staff and students of Jenks Southeast Elementary — model teachers who were teacher models! I'd also like to applaud Debbie Williams, a dream friend and teacher who is *still* speaking to me, even though I added an enormous behind to her pose in one of the illustrations. —K.D.

To the Teachers of America

In the hour of your death,
When others hear the voice of despair,
You will see the face of a child
And remember that you were a teacher.

Table of Contents

From the Author...

These poems are for the classroom teachers of America. I hope they make you laugh a lot and cry a little. I hope they help remind you of the power inherent in the art of teaching other human beings, the calling to which you have dedicated your lives. I hope that in each poem you discover a little of yourself.

In the classroom, teachers are isolated from their colleagues. I hope that reading these poems will give you the sense that you are not alone, that there are others who feel what you feel, and think what you think, and dream the dreams you may be tempted to abandon.

During the last 15 years as an author, I have visited hundreds of schools in all 50 states. At first, I believed I knew what it was to be a teacher. I was wrong. I knew very little. But I listened and I learned. Gradually, I began to experience a sense of reverence for teachers, and I think that's why I wrote these poems. I still do not understand what it is that gives you the courage and the generosity to do what you do, but I am honored to spend my life in your company.

So these poems are for you. I hope you enjoy them.

Brod Bagert

Prologue

The Answer Machine

She sat on the edge
Of a one-woman king-sized bed
And wondered if she could face another day.

Twenty-seven years in the classroom.

She tried not to think about it.
She tried not to remember her first-year-teacher dreams,
Dreams she had saved
Like the petals of a prom-corsage,
But now her tomorrows
Were heartbeats in a restless sleep
And dreams didn't matter anymore.

So with a sigh no one else could hear,
She readied pad and pencil
And pressed the play-back button
On her answer machine.

Hello Mrs. Stevenson,
This is Charlie MacWhite.
You probably don't remember me
But you taught me in the second grade,
I was the kid who still couldn't read.
Well I was thinking about you last night,
I was reading <u>Brown Bear</u> *to my little girl*
And it was strange
It was me saying the words…
But I kept hearing your voice in my head…
All these years
And your voice is still in my head.

Well I hope I didn't bother you,
But I just called to say you were right,
I did go to college,
And I did just fine,
And I wanted to say thank you…
Thanks for everything.

She sat on the edge
Of a one-woman king-sized bed,
Put pad and pencil down,
And smiled.

Twenty-seven years in the classroom…

Children, children, what do you see?
I see a *teacher* looking at me.

~ ACT ONE ~
The Children

The Threshold

I have opened lots of doors:
    Car doors, garage doors,
    Front doors, back doors,
    Ordinary doors and doors of leaded glass.
I have opened church doors
    To celebrate a wedding
    Or to mourn the death of a friend.
And I have opened doors I should have let stay closed.

But now,
This morning,
Here in the lower-school hallway,
I stand on a square of pea-green tile,
Worn through to the plywood underneath,
My hand clutches the doorknob,
And I hesitate,
For beyond this door
The future awaits me.
Twenty-three shiny-new kindergarteners,
Waiting for their one shiny-new kindergarten teacher.

Four years of college,
Ten thousand pages of instructional text,
A whirl of lectures that still swirl in my brain,
Yet nothing has prepared me for this.

I feel a little silly.
I can't stand here all day long.
After all, they're just children.
What could possibly go wrong?

Perfect Attendance

There was a child,
One of twenty-seven,
And this child never once sat still,
Never once behaved nicely,
And he never paid attention.
He talked, teased,
Played, piddled,
Argued and annoyed every creature
With whom he came into contact,
And he never missed a day of school!

Andrew Barneby Grimes.
Last year's Perfect Attendance Award recipient.

Strep throat?
Andrew came to school.

Eighteen inches of snow?
Andrew came to school.

A terrorist attack at the mall?
Andrew came to school,

And I am not surprised.
You see, Andrew's got a mamma,
And his mamma ain't no fool.
When you got a kid like Andrew…?
You *make* him go to school.

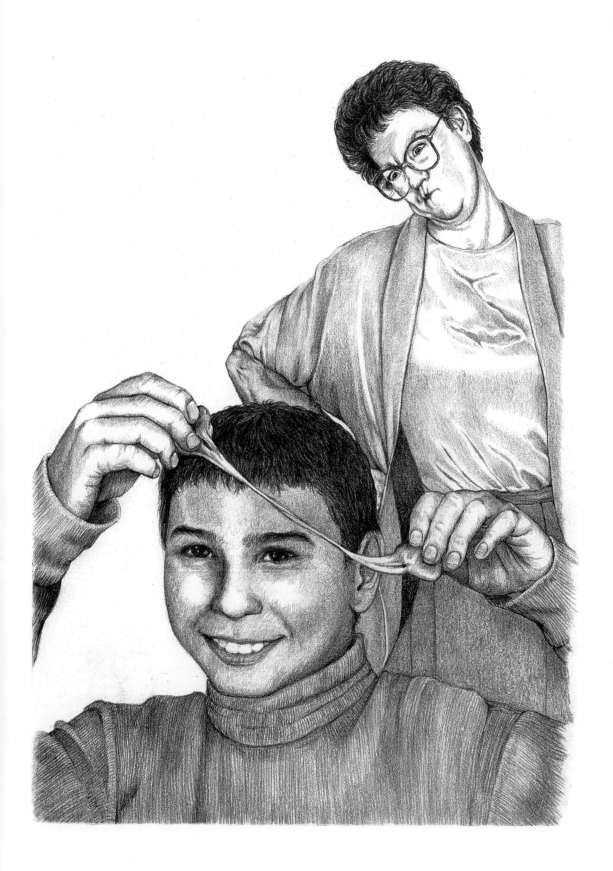

No Rush

In the first grade
Someone had called Homer a *slow learner*,
And he began to fear
He might never learn to read.
So they sent him to me
For one-on-one attention.

"You'll read," I promised.
"No need to worry,
No need to rush."
And we got started.
We worked… we played… we waited…
And Homer began to read.

Homer's in the fourth grade now,
And I had assumed he'd forgotten our sessions,
Until this morning
When I found his note slipped under my door.

The Reading Train
By Homer Pen

In a quiet little room,
With cozy Mrs. Lane,
I waited at the station
Till I caught the reading train.

At first the train moved slowly,
It was barely inching by,
But now it's time to buckle up,
This train is going to fly.

The Reading Train
by Homer Pen

In a quiet little room,
With cozy Mrs. Lane,
I waited at the station
Till I caught the reading train.

At first the train moved slowly,
It was barely inching by,
But now it's time to buckle up
This train is going to fly.

Homer Pen was afraid he might never learn to read,
But he isn't afraid anymore,
And nobody calls him a slow learner.

Straitjackets

With wild eyes
And a voice reed thin and brittle,
She whispered through the iron bars of a padded cell:

"I had everything under control —
    Thematic units,
    Bulletin boards,
    Child-centered seating,
And then they came,
Twenty-five small children,
Twenty-five children known now, far and wide,
As the second grade from hell!

"They should have come with a consumer warning…
They should have come with a cattle-prod!
Two hours…
It took two hours
To coax me out of the closet.
I stepped forth,
Wide-eyed and stunned,
As they wrapped long sleeves behind my back
And fastened leather straps.

"*Straightjackets!*
 I hissed.
That's what I needed all along.
Twenty-five, little-bitty straightjackets.

"Once it was all so different.
I had everything under control."

Hope for the Future

Her homework is neat.
Her projects are on time.
When I send her with the lunch count
She returns on time.
And during silent reading,
When I sit her next to terrible Tyrone,
She nods her understanding and never complains.

My wonderful little Megan —
Dependable, upright, and true.
If I wanted to clone a few more like her,
What would I have to do?

Metamorphosis

Third-grade angel,
Sixth-grade troll.
Three years can take
An awful toll.

The Special Ones

I watched him in the rear-view mirror
As he turned his siren off,
Alighted from his patrol car,
And, ticket book in hand,
Walked slowly toward me.

That's when I recognized him.
Virgil Jason Ryan!
Sixteen years ago
I was Virgil's fourth-grade teacher.
The faculty called him "Virge the Scourge"
And voted him most likely to go to the penitentiary,
And now he's a policeman
Standing at the window of my car.
He didn't get a word out of his mouth.
    "Virgil Ryan, how dare you!"
I growled.
    "I caught you cheating in math,
    I caught you lying about your homework,
    I caught you smoking in the bathroom,
    And if I hadn't cut you some slack,
    You'd still be in fourth grade,
    And you're going to give me a ticket
    For rolling slowly through a stop-sign."

By now I was out of the car,
Standing toe to toe,
And looking up at the bottom of his chin
As I lowered my voice to a snarl.
    "Now you listen to me, Virge the Scourge,
    And you listen good.
    Close that ticket book,
    And get back in your car,
    Or I'll send you home with a note to your mother."

"Mrs. Barker?" he said.
"Is that you?"
And he smiled,
"I'm sorry, Mrs. Barker.
I'll be good.
I'll never do it again."
Then he winked,
Gave me a hug…
And laughed all the way back to his car.

That Virgil…
He was always one of the special ones.

Justice of the Peace

I am not a judge.
Yet, I hear it every day —
    She won't let me play!
    He won't let me see!
    Tommy's making faces!
    He cut in front of me!

I smile sweetly and say:
    Now little people,
    Please try to share,
    Be nice to each other
    And always play fair.

What I do not say is:
    Now listen to me, you little vermin,
    If you don't stop this bickering,
    I'm going to lock you in the basement,
    Chain you to the wall,
    Feed you stale bread and grapefruit juice,
    And you'll never see your mothers again.

Oh to say it just one time!
To feel the sweet release!
But instead… I accept reality.
I'm the justice of the peace.

Child Mother

It was during morning hall duty,
As I stood at the doorway of my classroom.
   "I have to go home," she said,
   "My stomach hurts," she said,
   "I think there's something moving inside," she said,
And she trembled.

Eighth-grade eyes wet with tears,
Mary Elizabeth ahead of her years.

Child in spring... mother by fall...
Such big pain for a heart so small.

The Empty Desk

They say I have a gentle touch
And that's why they sent her to me.
So she spent her days in my classroom,
In the first desk of the third row.
     She listened,
     She learned,
     And she blossomed like a morning glory.

I can still remember her smile,
The day I stood beside her desk
As she pressed purple crayon to paper white
And ended the arch of her rainbow.

She spent her last days with me,
Right here in my classroom,
In this desk,
The first desk of the third row.

Because I have a gentle touch...
That's why they sent her to me.

Library-Gold

Jason Whitaker —
A name destined for the record books.
He's the fastest twelve-year-old in the state
And some say he's headed for Olympic gold,
But last week he stood in my library
And told me he hated to read.
"Books are for girls," he said, half-serious,
And headed for the track.

So this morning, in the hallway,
I witnessed a small miracle
When Jason,
His head buried in a book,
Walked directly into a wall.

I couldn't restrain a laugh,
And hearing me
He proffered the book by way of explanation.
"It's the one you gave me last week," he stammered.

"I see that," I answered,
And unable to resist I added,
"That one must be for boys."

If someday Jason wins the gold
I'll chèer him proud and tall,
But I'll cherish the memory of a boy with a book
Who walked into a wall.

Black and Blue

In fifteen years as the school counselor
She had received lots of subpoenas,
And now this one:
      Charmin vs. Charmin
    Hearing to Determine Custody
        Of a Minor Child.

That would be Ernie, she thought.
Seven-year-old Ernie
With the big brown eyes,
And the long curly lashes.

She spread the contents of Ernie's record on her desk —
His test results, her notes, and a drawing.
She could replay the day of that drawing like a video:
    "Ernie, make a picture of your family," she'd said.
    So, with a blue Crayon, Ernie drew a square.
    "That's a house," he explained.
    And then,
    With a black Crayon,
    He drew two stick figures,
    Each on opposite sides of the house.
    "That's Mommy and Daddy," he whispered.
And that was it.
Ernie's family portrait was complete.
There was no grass… no sun… no birds…
And no Ernie.

The little boy with lashes that curl,
Lost in a very lonely world.
The counselor of flesh and bone,
Wishing she were made of stone.

Discovery

"Marcus Jude steals things," they said.
"Watch him," they said,
"He stole from us,
And he'll steal from you."

But I knew better.
I knew that with patience and nurturing,
With love and understanding,
I could discover the good boy
Lost inside him.

So I was patient,
And I nurtured,
And I loved,
And I'm trying hard to understand
Why my paperweight was in his book-bag.
It was just a rock
With my name painted on it —
A gift from the children of my very first class,
Absolutely no value to anyone but me.

"Marcus Jude steals things," they said,
And now I know it's true.
Marcus stole from me,
And he will steal from you.

The Fire Makers

At dinner we discussed the evening news,
Politicians, movie stars, highly paid athletes,
But I noticed that one of the guests,
A teacher named Kanter,
Kept smiling to herself,
As though she had a secret,
And when I asked her about it,
She seemed embarrassed.

"It's really nothing," she said.
"I was thinking about math class today.
I wrote 3 x 5 = 15
And Donovan Graves looked at me
As if I had written $E = mc^2$.
So I explained:
    Three times five means
    Three equal groups of five,
    Like three nickels.
    If I give you three nickels,
    How much do you have?
I had explained it a hundred times before
But this time he got it.
One moment his eyes were mud
And the next moment there was fire.
It isn't a big thing
But I can't get it out of my head,
And when I think about it
I smile."

And smile she did,
And so did I.
You see,
Patsy Kanter's math lesson did not make the news,
But I am proud to say
That this evening,
I dined with a person
Who makes fire every day.

The Last Day of School

It's the roller-coaster day.
Everybody's excited about summer.
Everybody's sad to say goodbye.
We laugh a little,
We try not to cry,
And this year we held our tears
Until two twenty-seven PM,
And that is when she did it.

Clarisse St Marie!
Clarisse, who cried the first day of school —
    I want to go home.
Clarisse, who cried the entire first semester —
    I want to go home.
Clarisse, who broke all records
By crying one hundred seventy-nine consecutive days —
    I want to go home.

And today,
Day number one hundred and eighty,
The very last day of school,
Twenty three minutes before dismissal,
Clarisse cried again.

"Clarisse," we all shouted,
"Why do you grieve?"

"I'm crying," she said,
"Cause I don't want to leave."

And that's when it happened.
Our tears fell like rain.
I need this vacation.
I am going insane.

Summer Job

I didn't set the alarm last night.
I brushed my teeth,
Crawled into bed,
And slept till ten o'clock.
No papers to grade,
No PTA,
No early morning duty.
That's why they call it *summer vacation.*

But there's work to do this summer,
I'll get started on it soon.
This summer…?
I'm going to work real hard
To learn to sleep till noon.

~ ACT TWO ~
The Staff

Whirlwind

There was dark sky,
And brown grass,
And a narrow asphalt road
That stretched toward the horizon,
And above
A funnel cloud roared down to earth,
Turned into a snake,
And chased me into a dark wood…

And then I heard another sound,
From a different place:
    "Mamma, Tommy wet the bed again!"
And I am awake.
Friday, the twenty-first day of August.
Twelve days to Labor Day.
Thirteen days till the school year begins.
I lie awake in the bedroom of my home,
My poor little home
    With the windows I didn't wash this summer,
    With the attic I didn't organize
    With the floors I didn't strip,
    And walls that have not been painted
    Since Charles Lindberg landed in Paris.

Dirt and grime have won the day,
The whirlwind of summer has blown me away.

Two Tutors for an Engineer

"I could do your job," my husband said.
"Any day of the week,
I could walk into your classroom and teach math.
But you?
You could never do my job," he said.
Then he smiled smugly,
And went to sleep.

I did not smother him with a pillow.
I did however introduce him to two fourth grade children.
"Darling," I purred,
"Permit me to introduce you to Paul Stone and Jennifer Grip.
Perhaps you could help them with their long division."

I knew I could count on Jenny and Paul.
Paul is A.D.H.D. — Attention Deficit Hyperactive Disorder.
And Jenny?
She's L.O.V.E. — Totally gaga over Paul.
It was a thing of beauty.
The engineer barely escaped with his head.
Now every night he massages my feet,
And each morning I get breakfast in bed

Harmony in the Multipurpose Center

Dr. DiAngelo,
Holding his clarinet like a club,
Snarled and circled to his left.

Coach Martinez,
Holding her clipboard like a shield,
Growled and pivoted to face her foe.

"Band practice!" DiAngelo hissed.
"It says so on the schedule,
Thursday Afternoon — Band Practice!"

Martinez thundered back,
"When they made the schedule
We weren't in the playoffs yet.
Now we're there,
My team needs to practice,
And this gym is where we do it."

"Saturday is my Spring Concert,"
DiAngelo exploded,
"Three days to rehearse,
And besides…
It's not a gym!
It's a multipurpose center
And my purpose is as good as yours!"

It might have happened then and there,
A battle of gladiatorial proportions,
But it was averted by a single word.
J ... O ... C ... K.
That's right.
Dr. DiAngelo called Mrs. Martinez a *jock*.
More specifically,
He called her a *muscle-bound jock*.

Their laughter filled the room,
Hostility melted away,
And basketball with music
Co-existed for a day.

A Child Again

It was the day of our fall field trip
And spirits were high.
On the bus with my children,
I sat in the rear
And watched as the driver took her seat,
Glared into the rear-view mirror,
And bellowed,
    "No food,
      No feet in the aisle,
      No body parts out of the window."

So I,
A veteran teacher
With ten years in the classroom
And a master's degree,
Sat ramrod straight,

Pressed my lips together,
And stared directly ahead.

You see,
Mrs. Jones has driven this bus a long time,
And I remember a younger Mrs. Jones
Who slammed on the brakes,
Pointed her finger in my face
And shrieked:
    "I know your mother
    And I'm going to tell her
    Exactly what I saw you do."
I remember it as though it were yesterday,
And I'll never raise her wrath again —
This gargoyle of school bus strife!
When you're terrorized by Mrs. Jones,
You're terrorized for life.

The Note I Never Sent
To the Father of Martin Ambrose

Dear Mr. Ambrose,

Congratulations on the lovely job you did
With Martin's science project.
Your tree cross-section was accurate
And the root system was structurally correct.
Enclosed you will find Martin's version of the project.
I had him do it at school today.
It's not quite as detailed as yours
But it's very good.
You'll be happy to know
Martin earned a B.

Sincerely,
Norma Lester

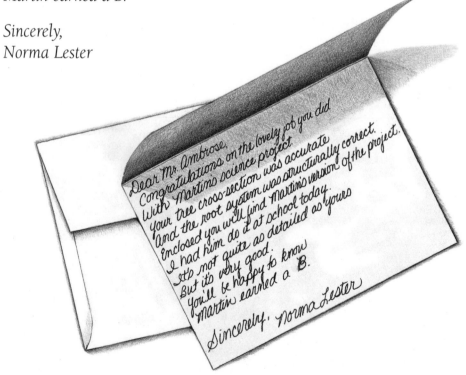

The Faculty Restroom Rule

The sole male member of the faculty,
Must remember the no-drip rule —
Always lift the toilet seat
When you use the john at school.

And remember, when you're finished...?
There are women all around,
So try to be a gentleman
And put the seat back down!

The Cafeteria

Grade B peanut butter,
Government surplus cheese,
Tacos with asparagus
And slimy yellow peas.

As they ladle out the food,
I smile with inner glee.
They can make the children eat it
But they can't make me.

A Prayer for Mr. Solomon Our School Custodian

The cafeteria was almost empty.
Most of the children had finished breakfast
And gone to class,
But seven-year-old Tanisia Jones had stayed behind,
And Mr. Solomon understood.
Sometimes Tanisia needs a little extra attention.

So he stopped his mop,
Frowned like a thunder cloud,
Stared down at tiny Tanisia Jones,
And growled:
    "Child,
    You just picking at that food.
    You better finish your breakfast
    Or I'm gonna pick on you."
The words sounded harsh
But Tanisia knew better,
And when she looked up
She was looking into the face of love.

Mr. Solomon has mopped the floor of this cafeteria
For as long as anyone remembers,
And nowhere in his job description will you find the words:
    Love and nurture children …
But that's what he does.
And if you ask him why
You'll hear him grumble:
    "If it weren't for those trifling children
    I'd have found me a better job thirty years ago."

Joe Solomon accepts no accolades.
He does what he does,
And he's done it for four decades.
And now he's starting to slow down.
So I hope the angels remember,
If heaven's got an entrance test…
No one gave more than Mr. Joseph Solomon,
And no one asked for less.

Burn Out

Helga Quinn Bickerson Thorn,
Loneliest teacher ever born.
A hermit-heart in a tower of stone,
Poor, poor Helga all alone.

"I'm tired of children," Helga said,
"Happy noises hurt my head.
Parents and teachers?
I'm tired of them too.
I'm tired of principals
And I'm tired of you."

Helga Quinn Bickerson Thorn,
Loneliest person ever born.
Chalk-dust dreams dry as bone,
Poor, poor Helga all alone.

The School Secretary

She held the phone to her ear
And spoke with deliberate calm.

"Listen closely, Mr. Klinger,
Because I want you to understand.
We challenged our children to read five thousand books,
And if they succeeded,
Our principal promised to spend Groundhog Day
Perched on a thirty-foot scaffold.
Now I'm happy to say
Our students exceeded their goal.
They read sixty-three hundred books,
We're all very proud
And our principal intends to keep his promise."

"You made a promise too, Mr. Klinger.
You promised to provide a thirty-foot scaffold,
And we paid you a deposit."

"Now tomorrow is Groundhog Day.
The children are excited,
The principal is willing,
And we will not disappoint them.
There will be no postponement,
There will be no delay,
You will erect a thirty-foot scaffold today,
And if there is anything you do not yet understand
I will be happy to have our attorney explain it to you."

Our principal works very hard,
And he's always on the run,
But at our school...? The secretary
Is the one who gets things done.

Head Lice

She manages prescription medication
For a score of children,
Applies first aid to everything
From compound-fractures to invisible booboos,
And tolerates the unpleasantness
Of spewed stomach-regurgitants.

Nurse Biddle,
A paragon of good cheer and professional poise...
Until today.

In the hallway,
Beside our Spring display of indigenous flowers,
Someone called my name,
And before I could respond
She had me.
    Wild-eyed and intense,
    She grabbed me by the ears,
    Jerked my chin to my chest,
    And with a wooden tongue-depressor
    Began to poke at my scalp.
    "They're everywhere..." she murmured.
    And before I could ascertain
    The identity of these ubiquitous invaders,
    She had pronounced me *clean*,
    And was rushing down the hall
    Toward an unsuspecting visitor,
    A dignified looking gentleman
    Whom I recognized immediately —
    The District Superintendent.

Nurse Biddle,
A dedicated health professional,
Faithful to the healer's pledge,
In the end it was the little things
That pushed her past the edge.

Camping Out

"This year, you'll be in a portable," she said,
"But it won't be for long," she promised.
"The new addition will be finished in June,
And next year you'll have a brand new classroom."

That's what she said,
Three years ago!
Three years of solitary confinement,
Three years of hiking through snow
To get to the toilet,
Three years of rain-soaked students,
Leaking roofs,
And wind howling through cracks!

The temporary portable classroom
Is a practical innovation,
But half the country's camping out
To get an education.

Rhinoceros Hide

A Conversation at the
State Reading Association

"Our principal is the ultimate micro-manager.
She alone makes every decision.
Last week we got a memo:
    Henceforth, at faculty meetings,
    There will be no potato chips,
    Instead we will serve corn chips.
    They stay fresh longer."

"We should have such problems.
Our principal never makes a decision.
It's his last year,
And he's counting the days to retirement."

"Well we've got Mr. Nice-guy.
He lets the children play Legos.
I send them to the office for discipline
And he makes it a reward."

At a recent meeting
Of the State Reading Association,
I listened to the conversation
And drew the following conclusion:

If your skin is not invincible
Please don't become the principal.

Big Sister

I have been observed.
At 1:17 PM.
Between Jonathan's wet pants
And Bianca's medication,
While teaching a lesson
On the life cycle of meal worms,
Just then —
    A movement at the door…
    My principal's face aglow…
    Her orange scarf aflow in her wake…
She enters,
Settles in the rear,
Smiles professionally,
And begins to observe me.
An INFORMAL observation.
An UNANNOUNCED INFORMAL observation.

Professional evaluation…
Isn't that a nice idea,
An idea I think we should spread around,
So how about this?
    Hello, Doctor,
    Don't let us interrupt your surgery.
    This is just an informal observation.
Or maybe…
    Good morning, Judge.
    Yes, it's that time again.
    I certainly hope your evaluation goes better this year.
Or perhaps…
    Pardon me, Mr. President,
    We seem to have caught you
    At an inopportune time.

Yes,
By all means,
Evaluation!
A sound idea and true.
But I think,
If you can check on me,
I get to check on you.

Ways and Means

How strange it is to see him here —
    Congressman J. Charles Witherford the Third,
    Known to his friends as *Side-Shuffle Charlie*,
    Powerful chairman of House Ways and Means,
    And confidante of four Presidents.
Now retired,
The congressman is a volunteer-reader at our school.
Every Tuesday and Thursday
I see him in the cafeteria
Reading to little Andy Roth,
And today,
Unable to resist any longer,
I introduced myself:
"My name is Debbie Abshire," I said,
"I'm Andy's teacher,
And I just wanted to say
What an honor it is to meet you,
And how wonderful it is
For you to volunteer your valuable time."

The congressman nodded graciously,
Shuffled one step to the side,
And began to speak in that warm growl
I had heard so often on television.
    "For twenty-one years
    I walked the halls of political power.
    I was wined, dinned, maligned, and revered,
    Yet each night,
    When I put my head on the pillow,
    I felt the ooze of futility
    Like tar in the marrow of my bones.
    But tonight I'm going to sleep like a baby.
    My valuable time,' you say,
    And for the first time in my life I agree,
    The time I spend reading to this child
    Is indeed a thing of value."
Then he stood erect,
Took my hand in his,
And whispered,
    "So you see, Ms. Abshire,
    It is I who am honored to meet you."

Rambo Teacher

At the parents' meeting the other day
I could hardly believe what I heard them say.
 We don't want our children getting any new ideas,
 So please, just drill the basics and satisfy our fears.
 All they need is phonics rules
 To make them learn to read,
 Phonics rules and ditto sheets
 Until their fingers bleed!
Oh-me-oh-my, oh what to do?
Can I do what's right and please them too?
I've always been a gentle creature,
This is a job for Rambo Teacher!
  Rambo Teachers know what's right,
  Rambo Teachers stand and fight,
  They always put the children first
  And cultivate their learning thirst.

At the school board meeting the other day
I could hardly believe what I heard them say.
 You teachers better listen, we're the ones who write your check,
 And I'm about to tell you the results that we expect.
 The competition's tough.
 We have to be the best.
 Just teach those kids to get high scores
 On the state achievement test.
Oh-me-oh-my, oh what to do?
Can I do what's right and please them too?
I've always been a peaceful creature,
This is a job for Rambo Teacher.
  Rambo Teachers know what's right,
  Rambo Teachers stand and fight,
  They always put the children first
  And cultivate their learning thirst.

I work with children every day
And this is what I hear them say.
Oh teacher, teacher, save us please!
We need your help, we're on our knees.
We're little kids and school's a jail.
Don't make us live afraid to fail.
When you read us poems and stories
Our imaginations burn.
Just trust us and you'll see,
We really love to learn.
Oh-me-oh-my…
Oh what to do?
Can I please all of them and be true to you?
That's it!
I've had it up to here!
I will no longer live in fear!
I used to be a gentle creature
But hold on world
I'm Rambo Teacher!
Rambo Teachers know what's right!
Rambo Teachers stand and fight!
They can say what they will and do what they must
But we've given our lives and we've earned their trust.
We always put the children first.
We cultivate their learning thirst.

Epilogue

The Sand Walker

With hair in the wind
And ears for the sea
And eyes that owned the world
She stood barefoot on the sand
And fed sea gulls.

They bobbed on the air above her
And swooped down
Each time she tossed bread into the sky
And when she had nothing left to give
They flew away.

I watched her on an afternoon.
I had seen her face
And beheld the movement of her body
And followed her foot steps
To where they disappeared in the waves.

I look for her now.
I watch the water and wait
But I do not think she will return.
Yet I am sure another will come,
Someone who will stand the wind,
Someone else whose feet are bare
Will walk the sand
And feed children in the air.

Acknowledgments

The idea for this book began with Joan Stevenson, a retired teacher who manages a children's book store in South Carolina. She said we needed a collection of poems for teachers and suggested I write it.

She told me of a message she received from a former student. She said it was the kind of experience teachers live for and that it would be a good place to start. A year and a half later, after a dozen false starts, I found a voice that felt authentic and wrote the poem, "The Answer Machine."

During the next year I managed to write a few more poems and was encouraged when I shared them with teachers. I was in unfamiliar territory and teacher reaction began to serve as a compass to keep me on the path. I became particularly dependent on a group of incredible teachers in rural Oklahoma — Jayne Cox, Marilyn Denison, Donna Lane, Lisa Lawrence, and the formidable Cathy Barker, godmother of this book and inspiration for the poem, "The Special Ones." My own faith in the project began to grow as I began to see the poems through their eyes.

When the manuscript was ready for a publisher, fate introduced me to the visionary Julia Graddy of Maupin House. Julia has a gift for understanding the needs of teachers and, under her leadership, Maupin House is destined to become a leader in professional publishing for educators.

I'd also like to thank my third-grade teacher, Mrs. Toups, who planted the seed of poetry in my heart and died before it sprouted; Gary Esolen, whose knowledge of poetry is a light in the darkness; Cindy Elliot and the teachers of Louisiana, who believed I had something to give and refused to let me ignore it; Debbie Abshire who taught me that my work could cross state lines; Bernice "Ms. Bee" Cullinan, one of the twentieth century's great women, who believed in an unknown poet; Kent Brown, who gave me a start in the world of publishing; Bill Martin Jr., whose love for teachers and children is the ideal I try to imitate; Mike Sampson of Pathways to Literacy, whose faith gave my work much-needed exposure and provided the incubator for my appreciation of teachers; and Tommy Thomason, my writing coach.

Thanks also to the many teachers and conference coordinators in 50 states and two territories who found me in the tar pit of the courtroom and invited me to their island of dedication and accomplishment, the like of which I did not know existed and only now am beginning to understand.

I also send thanks to my mom, who speaks spontaneous poetry; and to my dad, who on a thousand occasions made me find in the dictionary the word "perseverance" and read to him out loud its definition.

And finally, thanks to my wife, Debby, the strong and beautiful woman who, when her husband left a 21-year law practice to become a poet, stood firmly beside him, picked up the financial slack, and made possible the miracle of his life; and to our four wonderful children, who never doubted.

About the Author and Illustrator

Brod Bagert

Like a poetic Johnny Appleseed, Brod Bagert travels America, visiting schools and conferences with the message that poetry comes alive for children when they perform it. His own poems are often funny, sometimes sad, and always highly performable. Brod has published fifteen books of poetry for children and adults and has developed a technique for teaching poetry which he calls the Performance Method. He says of **Rainbows, Head Lice and Pea-Green Tile**, "This one's for the teachers — my own heroes."

Kim Doner

Photo: Jimmy Bloyed

Illustrator Kim Doner knows how to draw a good story — whether it's for a poster, magazine illustration, or book. Kim's second illustrated book, *Green Snake Ceremony*, won her the Oklahoma Book Award for Best Illustrated Book. Her latest book, *Buffalo Dreams*, marks her debut as a writer as well as an illustrator. Between book deadlines, the versatile Kim makes humor-filled and inspiring visits to schools and conferences, sharing the joyous journey of a creative concept from idea to reality.